The Unexpected Millionaire

How Anyone Can Build Massive Wealth by Identifying and Investing in Overlooked Local Businesses

BY
Jagger Cobair

CONTENTS

INTRODUCTION 1
Discovering the Hidden Path to Wealth 2

Part 1: 9
Laying the Foundation 9

Chapter 01 10
Understanding the Local Business Landscape 10
Chapter 02 19
The Power of Community-Driven Wealth 19
Chapter 03 28
The Mindset of an Unexpected Millionaire 28

PART 2: 36
Identifying the Right Opportunities 36

Chapter 04 37
Finding Hidden Gems in Your Community 37
Chapter 05 46
Doing Your Homework 46
Chapter 06 54
Creating an Opportunity Funnel 54

Part 3: 62
Investing and Growing Wealth 62

Chapter 07 63
The Art of Making the Deal 63
.... 63
Chapter 08 72
Managing Your Investment Effectively 72

Chapter 09 81
Scaling Up for Bigger Wins 81

Part 4: 89
Long-Term Strategies for Wealth 89

Chapter 10 90
Building a Legacy Through Local Investments 90
Chapter 11 97
Learning From Setbacks and Failures 97
Chapter 12 105
Celebrating Success and Staying Grounded 105

Conclusion 112
The Journey From Ordinary to Extraordinary 113

INTRODUCTION

Discovering the Hidden Path to Wealth

Why Most People Miss Millionaire Opportunities

When we hear the term "millionaire," it often conjures images of tech moguls, Wall Street traders, or celebrities living lives of glamour. These stereotypes create a mental barrier for many of us. We start believing that wealth is reserved for the exceptionally talented, highly educated, or well-connected. The truth, however, is far less exclusive. Opportunities to build wealth exist all around us, but they often go unnoticed or unrecognized. Why? Because they rarely look glamorous at first glance.

The Blind Spots That Hold People Back

Overlooking Small Beginnings:
Many assume wealth requires a grand idea or significant investment upfront. Yet, the reality is that most millionaires start small — often with just a willingness to learn and work hard.

Belief in Quick Riches:
The allure of get-rich-quick schemes diverts focus from sustainable wealth-building. These promises are tempting, but they lead to dead ends or financial losses more often than success.

Fear of the Unknown:
Most people fear stepping out of their comfort zone. They avoid taking calculated risks or trying something

unconventional, preferring to stick with the predictable, even if it's unfulfilling.

Misguided Definitions of Wealth:
True wealth is not just financial. It's about freedom, opportunities, and the ability to shape your future. When people focus solely on money, they often miss the broader picture and pathways to lasting success.

The Myths About Wealth-Building That Hold People Back

Misconceptions about wealth-building are among the biggest obstacles to financial success. Let's break some of these myths so we can start on a clean slate.

Myth #1: "You Need Money to Make Money"
While initial capital can help, many millionaires began with little or no money. They leveraged knowledge, relationships, and creativity instead of focusing on their lack of resources.

Myth #2: "Only Risk-Takers Become Millionaires"
Wealth-building does involve risk, but it's not about reckless gambling. Unexpected millionaires succeed by taking calculated, manageable risks—not betting everything on a single idea.

Myth #3: "Wealth is for the Young"
Starting late doesn't disqualify you from financial success. Many individuals achieved their first million

well into their 40s, 50s, or even later, proving age is no barrier.

Myth #4: "Education Guarantees Wealth"

While education can be an asset, it is not the sole determinant of success. Many unexpected millionaires thrive by being street-smart, resourceful, and action-oriented, regardless of formal degrees.

The Concept of Unexpected Millionaires

What sets the "unexpected millionaire" apart? These are individuals who defy conventional wisdom about wealth creation. They don't follow the typical paths of high-paying jobs or large investments. Instead, they:

Spot Hidden Opportunities: They find value where others see none. For instance, a small-town bakery owner who innovates their menu can turn a local business into a thriving success story.

Stay Persistent: Unexpected millionaires embrace consistent effort, knowing small actions over time yield significant results.

Adapt and Innovate: They don't let circumstances dictate their future. Whether it's learning a new skill or entering an unfamiliar industry, they adapt quickly to seize opportunities.

Stories of Ordinary Individuals Who Found Wealth in Surprising Places

Case Study 1: From Hobby to Empire

John, a high school teacher, began making custom wooden furniture in his garage as a stress-relief hobby. He posted photos on social media, and within months, he had more orders than he could handle. John scaled his operations and, five years later, sold his business for $2 million.

Case Study 2: The Farmer Who Marketed Differently

Maria, a small-town farmer, noticed that tourists loved local products. She rebranded her farm as a "rustic getaway," offering farm tours and artisanal goods. Her small farm became a regional attraction, turning a modest profit into six figures annually.

Case Study 3: The Digital Side Hustler

Liam, a stay-at-home dad, taught himself graphic design through free online tutorials. He started freelancing part-time, building a clientele through referrals. Within three years, Liam was running his own agency, earning over $500,000 a year.

These stories share a common thread: the path to wealth doesn't require revolutionary ideas—it requires consistent action and a willingness to think differently.

Why Local Businesses Are the Best Kept Secret

One of the most underrated avenues for building wealth is local business. These opportunities often fly under the radar, overshadowed by the hype of online startups or stock market investments. Yet, they remain an accessible and steady route to financial independence.

The Advantages of Local Businesses

Close Connections to the Community:
Local businesses thrive on relationships. Building trust with your community often leads to loyal customers and organic growth.

Lower Entry Barriers:
Unlike tech startups that demand coding skills or substantial capital, many local businesses can be started with minimal expertise or investment.

Recession-Resistant Opportunities:
Businesses like food services, repair shops, and childcare tend to survive economic downturns because they meet essential needs.

Potential for Innovation:
Even traditional businesses can stand out with fresh ideas. A laundromat that offers eco-friendly services or a bookstore that doubles as a café can attract modern customers.

What This Book Will Teach You

This guide is not about abstract theories or unattainable goals. It's a practical roadmap designed to help you find wealth where you least expect it. By the end, you will have:

Clarity on Your Goals: Learn to identify what wealth means for you—freedom, security, or impact—and tailor your approach accordingly.

A Step-by-Step Process: Discover actionable methods to identify and capitalize on overlooked local business opportunities.

The Tools to Overcome Barriers: Learn to navigate challenges like limited capital, lack of experience, or fear of failure.

Inspiration to Start Small: Understand how small steps can lead to big outcomes over time.

This book doesn't promise overnight success, but it will arm you with the strategies to achieve lasting financial independence.

Who Can Benefit From This Guide

The beauty of this path is that it's for everyone. Whether you're a stay-at-home parent, a retiree, a recent graduate, or someone starting over, the principles in this book apply universally. Here's why:

You Don't Need a Fancy Degree:
Resourcefulness often trumps academic credentials in the local business landscape.

You Don't Need a Fortune to Start:
Many of the examples in this book involve starting with as little as $100—or even just an idea.

You Don't Need Youth or Time on Your Side:
It's never too late to begin. What matters is commitment and consistency.

You Don't Need Perfect Circumstances:
Life is messy, but wealth-building doesn't require perfection. It requires effort, adaptability, and courage.

Final Thoughts on Starting Your Journey

Wealth doesn't have to be a distant dream. It's often closer than you think, hidden in your community or within your existing skills. The journey to becoming an unexpected millionaire starts with small, consistent steps. Are you ready to take the first one?

Part 1: Laying the Foundation

Chapter 01

Understanding the Local Business Landscape

To lay the groundwork for wealth-building through local businesses, we must first understand what makes these opportunities so special. Local businesses are the lifeblood of communities, often overlooked yet brimming with potential. They offer accessible avenues for ordinary people to achieve extraordinary success.

What Defines a Local Business?

At its core, a local business is one that primarily serves a specific community or region. These businesses operate on a smaller scale than national or multinational corporations, focusing on personal connections and localized services. But don't mistake their size for lack of impact—many local businesses punch far above their weight.

Key Characteristics of Local Businesses

Community-Centric:
Local businesses are deeply embedded in their communities. Whether it's a neighborhood café or a family-run hardware store, their success often hinges on trust and reputation.

Smaller Scale Operations:
These businesses typically have fewer employees and operate out of a single or limited number of locations, keeping overhead manageable.

Personalized Customer Service:
Unlike large corporations, local businesses thrive on offering tailored experiences, fostering customer loyalty.

Flexibility and Adaptability:
Local entrepreneurs can pivot quickly to meet market demands—whether it's introducing new products or embracing technology.

Direct Owner Involvement:
Owners are often hands-on, building relationships with customers and keeping operations efficient.

Types of Businesses to Consider and Their Common Characteristics

When exploring the local business landscape, the possibilities are vast. Here are some types of businesses that tend to thrive and their distinguishing traits:

1. Food and Beverage

From bakeries to food trucks, the food industry is a perennial favorite for local entrepreneurs.

- **Low Startup Costs**: Many food businesses can begin as home-based operations or pop-ups.
- **Recession-Resilient**: People always need to eat, ensuring consistent demand.
- **Potential for Innovation**: Unique menus or locally sourced ingredients can set a business apart.

2. Personal Services

These include beauty salons, fitness trainers, and repair services.

- **Community Loyalty**: Personal relationships drive repeat business.
- **Scalability**: Once established, these services can expand through additional locations or franchising.

3. Retail

Small shops selling clothes, home goods, or artisanal products.

- **Uniqueness**: Offering niche or locally crafted items creates a competitive edge.
- **Integration with E-commerce**: Many local retailers can broaden their reach online.

4. Professional Services

Accounting firms, legal services, or consulting businesses.

- **Expertise-Driven**: Success often relies on specialized skills or knowledge.
- **Stable Demand**: These services are needed across all economic cycles.

5. Manufacturing or Production

Small-scale producers of furniture, candles, or even specialty foods.

- **Focus on Quality**: Handmade or locally produced items often fetch a premium.

> **Sustainability Appeal**: Consumers increasingly value eco-friendly practices.

Why Local Businesses Are Often Overlooked

Despite their potential, local businesses often fail to attract the attention they deserve. This neglect stems from a variety of biases and misconceptions.

1. The Glamour of Big Names

People are drawn to well-known brands or tech startups, associating them with prestige and success. As a result, smaller, less flashy opportunities in the local sphere are undervalued.

2. Assumptions About Scalability

The misconception that local businesses can't grow or generate significant revenue keeps many potential investors and entrepreneurs away.

3. Lack of Visibility

Small businesses often lack the marketing budgets of larger companies, making them less noticeable to potential customers or investors.

4. Fear of Saturation

Many people mistakenly believe their local market is too small or saturated for new businesses to thrive. In reality, even crowded markets often have unmet needs waiting to be addressed.

Local Businesses vs. Big Corporations

While it's easy to assume that big corporations dominate every market, local businesses have several unique advantages that allow them to compete and often outperform their larger counterparts.

Key Advantages of Local Businesses

Personalized Customer Experience:
Small businesses can offer a level of service and personalization that big companies struggle to replicate. Knowing customers by name or offering custom solutions builds loyalty.

Community Trust:
Local businesses are more likely to gain the trust of their community, leading to repeat customers and word-of-mouth referrals.

Flexibility:
Big corporations are like ocean liners—hard to steer quickly. Local businesses, by contrast, are nimble speedboats. They can adapt to new trends or customer needs almost instantly.

Lower Overheads:
Smaller operations often mean reduced costs, allowing local businesses to operate profitably even with modest revenue.

Creative Freedom:
Owners of local businesses have full control over their

operations. This freedom encourages innovation, whether it's introducing unique product lines or embracing sustainable practices.

Examples of Overlooked Local Businesses That Flourish

Let's explore real-world examples of small, overlooked businesses that became powerful engines of wealth.

1. The Corner Coffee Shop

Lisa opened a small café in her neighborhood, focusing on locally roasted coffee and hosting open mic nights. Over time, it became a community hub. With minimal marketing, her café doubled its revenue each year, allowing her to open two more locations.

2. The Family Cleaning Service

After losing his corporate job, James started a small cleaning service with his family. By targeting busy professionals and offering eco-friendly cleaning options, James turned his venture into a six-figure business within three years.

3. The Local Crafter

Sara, a stay-at-home mom, began making handmade soap for fun. When friends started buying her creations, she expanded her efforts, eventually landing her products in local stores and online marketplaces.

These examples illustrate that wealth is not reserved for the tech giants or Wall Street insiders — it's achievable for everyday people willing to put in the effort.

Trends and Changes in Local Markets

Markets are constantly evolving, and successful entrepreneurs keep an eye on trends to seize new opportunities. Here's what to watch for:

1. The Rise of Sustainability

Consumers increasingly prefer eco-friendly and sustainable products. Businesses that cater to this demand, like refill stations for household products or upcycled clothing stores, are thriving.

2. Digital Integration

Even local businesses are embracing online tools to expand their reach. From offering delivery through apps to marketing on social media, digital integration is no longer optional.

3. Health and Wellness Boom

There's growing interest in health-conscious products and services, from organic food to fitness classes. Local businesses can capitalize on this trend by offering tailored solutions.

4. Niche Markets

Specialized businesses serving unique needs—like gluten-free bakeries or pet grooming salons—are seeing growing demand.

5. Work-From-Home Economy

With more people working remotely, there's a surge in demand for services like coworking spaces, delivery solutions, and home office setup businesses.

Key Takeaways

Understanding the local business landscape reveals a world of untapped opportunities. By recognizing the unique strengths of small businesses and staying attuned to changing market trends, you can position yourself to succeed. Whether you're starting from scratch or looking to invest, the potential is right in front of you—all it takes is the willingness to see it.

Chapter 02

The Power of Community-Driven Wealth

When it comes to building wealth through local businesses, the community is not just a backdrop—it's the lifeblood. The relationship between a thriving local economy and individual financial success is deeply intertwined. By understanding and leveraging the power of community-driven wealth, you not only secure personal gains but also create a lasting positive impact for others around you.

The Role of Community in Local Business Success

A Symbiotic Relationship

Local businesses and their communities exist in a mutually beneficial relationship. When a business succeeds, it feeds the local economy, creating jobs, fostering innovation, and improving quality of life. In return, the community's trust and support provide the foundation for that business's growth.

Economic Flow:
A dollar spent at a local business circulates within the community, generating more wealth and supporting other local businesses. This multiplier effect strengthens the economic ecosystem.

Cultural Identity:
Local businesses contribute to the unique identity of a community. Whether it's the corner diner or the family-run boutique, these establishments become landmarks that foster pride and belonging.

Problem Solvers: Small businesses often address local needs that larger corporations overlook, from niche services to personalized care. In doing so, they create value and deepen their connection with the community.

How Investing Locally Benefits You and Others

Investing locally offers a win-win proposition: you grow your wealth while helping to strengthen the community you call home. Here's how it works:

1. A Stronger Local Economy

By putting money into local businesses—whether as a customer, investor, or partner—you directly contribute to your community's economic health. Strong local economies attract more talent, innovation, and resources, increasing opportunities for everyone.

> **Example**: Funding a neighborhood coworking space can help freelancers and entrepreneurs in your area succeed, boosting overall prosperity.

2. Personal Satisfaction and Connection

Unlike anonymous investments in stocks or large corporations, supporting local businesses creates tangible, visible results. Watching a local café you supported thrive or seeing neighbors employed by a business you helped fund brings a sense of accomplishment.

3. Higher ROI Potential

Local investments often offer a more significant return on investment compared to traditional financial products. You're dealing directly with the business owner, cutting out intermediaries and gaining a more personalized relationship with your investment.

Trust, Loyalty, and Local Business Owners

Building Relationships for Success

In the local business landscape, relationships are everything. Trust and loyalty aren't just abstract concepts—they translate into tangible benefits like customer retention, referrals, and long-term partnerships.

Why Trust Matters

1. **Word of Mouth is Gold**:
   Customers who trust you will not only return but also recommend your business to friends and family.
2. **Stronger Partnerships**:
   Business relationships built on trust lead to collaborations that benefit everyone involved.

How to Build Trust as a Business Owner

➢ **Show Up Consistently**: Reliability is the cornerstone of trust. Meet deadlines, honor commitments, and be a dependable presence in your community.

- **Engage Authentically**: Get involved in local events, support causes that matter to your customers, and make genuine connections.
- **Deliver Quality**: Trust is built on a track record of excellence. Consistently exceeding expectations solidifies your reputation.

Loyalty: The Secret Ingredient to Growth

Loyal customers are the backbone of any local business. Their repeat business provides a stable revenue stream, while their advocacy helps you grow.

- **Personalized Service**: Local businesses often excel at tailoring experiences to their customers, creating deep emotional connections.
- **Exclusive Perks**: Offering loyalty programs or special perks fosters a sense of exclusivity, turning casual customers into brand ambassadors.

The Ripple Effect of Supporting Local Entrepreneurs

Supporting local businesses is like planting a tree in your backyard—it benefits you immediately, but its long-term impact spreads far beyond your initial investment.

Economic Ripple Effects

When you support a local entrepreneur, you create a chain reaction of benefits:

1. **Job Creation**: Small businesses are significant job creators, offering opportunities to people in your community.
2. **Wealth Circulation**: Dollars spent locally are reinvested into other local businesses, schools, and infrastructure.
3. **Reduced Economic Leakage**: Unlike national chains that send profits to distant headquarters, local businesses keep money within the community.

Social Ripple Effects

Local businesses do more than generate wealth; they enrich the social fabric of your community.

- **Fostering Innovation**: Entrepreneurs often bring fresh ideas and unique products to the table, improving the community's overall quality of life.
- **Building Connections**: A thriving local economy encourages residents to shop, dine, and engage locally, creating stronger interpersonal ties.

Environmental Ripple Effects

Local businesses often source their materials and labor close to home, reducing their carbon footprint. Additionally, they're more likely to invest in sustainable practices that benefit the environment.

Spotting Win-Win Investment Opportunities

To maximize the benefits of local investing, look for opportunities where everyone involved can thrive. Here's how to identify these win-win scenarios:

1. Focus on Underserved Needs

Successful investments often fill gaps in the market. Look for businesses that solve specific problems for your community.

- ➤ **Example**: If your area lacks affordable childcare, funding a daycare center could provide both a financial return and a vital service.

2. Evaluate Community Impact

Choose investments that positively impact the community, such as job creation, skill development, or improved access to essential goods and services.

- ➤ **Example**: Investing in a local farmer's market supports farmers while providing fresh produce to residents.

3. Partner with Passionate Entrepreneurs

The best local investments are driven by people who are deeply committed to their vision. Look for business owners with a strong work ethic, clear goals, and a connection to the community.

- ➤ **Example**: A baker who dreams of expanding her shop to offer classes for aspiring pastry chefs is likely to bring passion and purpose to her work.

4. Seek Scalable Ventures

While not every local business will expand into a national chain, some have the potential for significant growth. Consider how a business could scale through franchising, e-commerce, or partnerships.

> **Example**: A boutique specializing in handcrafted jewelry might gain traction through an online store.

5. Evaluate Risk and Reward

Local investments often carry less risk than high-stakes ventures like tech startups, but it's still essential to assess potential challenges. Look for businesses with clear plans, manageable debt, and strong community support.

Final Thoughts on the Power of Community-Driven Wealth

Wealth is not built in isolation—it thrives on connection. By supporting local businesses and embracing community-driven wealth, you not only improve your financial standing but also play a crucial role in creating a stronger, more resilient local economy. Every dollar spent or invested locally has the power to transform lives, uplift neighborhoods, and create a ripple effect of positivity.

Your path to unexpected wealth doesn't require reinventing the wheel. It begins with recognizing the opportunities right in front of you and nurturing the community that supports them. In doing so, you build something far greater than individual success—you contribute to a legacy of shared prosperity.

Chapter 03

The Mindset of an Unexpected Millionaire

Wealth-building begins in the mind. While strategies and opportunities are essential, a millionaire mindset transforms how you approach money, risk, and opportunity. In this chapter, we explore the mental shifts required to transition from financial struggle to financial success, even in unexpected places.

Shifting from Consumer to Investor

One of the first steps to adopting the mindset of an unexpected millionaire is recognizing the difference between being a consumer and an investor. Most people spend their lives consuming—spending money on things that lose value over time. Millionaires think differently: they prioritize investments that grow wealth instead of depleting it.

Identifying Counterproductive Spending Habits

Excessive consumption doesn't just drain your bank account—it blinds you to opportunities for growth. Here are some common habits to watch for:

1. **Impulse Purchases**: Frequently buying items you don't need on a whim.
2. **Lifestyle Inflation**: Spending more as your income increases, rather than saving or investing the difference.
3. **Unexamined Subscriptions**: Paying monthly for services or memberships you rarely use.

Redirecting Spending into Investments

Every dollar has the potential to multiply if allocated wisely. Begin shifting your focus from "How can I spend?" to "How can I grow?"

- **Start Small**: Redirect the money you'd spend on unnecessary luxuries into savings or low-risk investments.
- **Reinvest in Yourself**: Use funds to learn a new skill, attend networking events, or develop a side business.
- **Focus on Assets, Not Liabilities**: Buy things that generate income, such as equipment for a side hustle or shares in a local business.

Thinking Long-Term in a Short-Term World

We live in a culture obsessed with instant gratification. From fast food to overnight delivery, we're conditioned to expect immediate results. However, wealth-building demands a long-term mindset.

The Power of Patience

Success doesn't happen overnight, and the journey to becoming an unexpected millionaire is no exception. Long-term thinking allows you to:

1. **Avoid Rash Decisions**: Taking time to evaluate investments reduces the likelihood of costly mistakes.

2. **Leverage Compounding**: Whether it's financial interest or accumulated expertise, small gains over time lead to exponential growth.
3. **Weather Economic Cycles**: By focusing on the big picture, you can navigate market downturns without panic.

Strategies to Develop Long-Term Thinking

- **Set Clear Goals**: Write down where you want to be financially in 5, 10, and 20 years. Use these goals as a guide for daily decisions.
- **Celebrate Progress**: Acknowledge milestones along the way to keep your motivation high.
- **Delay Gratification**: Practice saying "no" to short-term pleasures that detract from your long-term plans.

Overcoming Fear of Small Business Risk

Fear is one of the most significant barriers to action. Many potential millionaires avoid investing in local businesses because they perceive them as too risky. While some risk is inherent, most can be managed with preparation and a proactive approach.

Common Fears and Their Solutions

1. **Fear of Financial Loss**:

- **Solution**: Start small. Only invest what you can afford to lose while you gain experience.

2. **Fear of Failure:**

   ➤ **Solution:** Redefine failure as feedback. Every setback is an opportunity to learn and improve.

3. **Fear of the Unknown:**

   ➤ **Solution:** Research thoroughly. Understanding a business, market, and community significantly reduces uncertainty.

Practical Ways to Build Confidence

➤ **Study Similar Successes:** Learn from others who started small and achieved significant growth.
➤ **Partner with Experts:** Collaborate with people who have experience in the business you're exploring.
➤ **Create a Safety Net:** Maintain an emergency fund to reduce anxiety about potential losses.

Embracing Curiosity and Observation

Opportunities for wealth often appear in plain sight—but only to those willing to look. Curiosity and observation are key traits of unexpected millionaires. Developing these skills allows you to recognize untapped potential that others ignore.

How to Train Your Eyes for Opportunity

Ask Questions: Cultivate the habit of asking "Why?" and "What if?"

- Why is this business thriving?
- What if I improved this product or service?

Engage with Your Community: The best insights come from listening to people's needs and frustrations. Conversations with customers, neighbors, and friends can reveal hidden gaps in the market.

Notice Trends: Pay attention to emerging behaviors, such as shifts in spending habits or growing interest in specific products. For example:

- Increased demand for eco-friendly solutions.
- Growth in remote work and home-based services.

Curiosity in Action

- **Example 1**: A local entrepreneur noticed the growing popularity of meal prep services but saw no providers in her town. By starting her own, she built a thriving business.
- **Example 2**: A handyman observed that elderly residents struggled with minor home repairs. He began offering affordable assistance and quickly became the go-to expert in his community.

Building Resilience Through Failure

Every success story includes failures along the way. The difference between those who succeed and those who don't is resilience. Millionaires don't see failure as the end—they see it as a step toward their goals.

The Value of Failure

1. **Clarifies Your Path**: Setbacks force you to reevaluate and refine your strategies.
2. **Builds Emotional Strength**: Learning to handle disappointment prepares you for future challenges.
3. **Inspires Innovation**: Many breakthroughs occur when you're forced to adapt to unforeseen obstacles.

Strategies to Turn Failures into Lessons

- **Reflect, Don't Dwell**: After a setback, ask yourself:

✓ What went wrong?
✓ What can I do differently next time?

- **Seek Support**: Surround yourself with mentors or peers who can offer advice and encouragement.
- **Celebrate Attempts**: Even if you don't succeed, acknowledge the courage it took to try. Every effort brings you closer to mastery.

Resilience in Action

- **Example**: A restaurant owner faced a sudden drop in business during an economic downturn. Instead of giving up, she pivoted to offering takeout and catering services, eventually surpassing her previous revenue.

Final Thoughts on the Millionaire Mindset

The journey to becoming an unexpected millionaire doesn't begin with a bank account—it begins with a mindset. By shifting from consumer to investor, thinking long-term, managing risk, cultivating curiosity, and embracing failure, you can unlock your potential to find wealth in the most unexpected places.

The road isn't always easy, but each challenge you overcome strengthens your foundation for lasting success. The key is to act boldly, stay persistent, and always keep your eyes open for the next opportunity. Your millionaire mindset is the compass that will guide you there.

PART 2: Identifying the Right Opportunities

Chapter 04
Finding Hidden Gems in Your Community

Opportunities for financial success often exist right under your nose. Hidden gems—overlooked or undervalued businesses—are abundant in every community, waiting for someone with the vision to recognize their potential. This chapter explores how to uncover these opportunities and assess their viability.

Where to Look for Overlooked Businesses

Finding hidden gems requires stepping outside your usual routine and exploring your community with fresh eyes. Here are practical places to start your search:

1. Local Directories and Listings

- **Chamber of Commerce Websites**: These often list small businesses, many of which are family-owned and may not have robust marketing.
- **Local Business Directories**: Look for online platforms like Yelp or niche directories specific to your area.
- **Classified Ads**: Check local newspapers or online marketplaces for businesses looking to sell or expand.

2. Community Boards and Social Media

- **Community Bulletin Boards**: Found in libraries, grocery stores, or coffee shops, these boards often feature services or businesses looking for customers or collaborators.
- **Facebook Groups**: Many towns and neighborhoods have dedicated groups for small

business discussions, recommendations, and promotions.

3. Networking Events

- **Local Meetups**: Business-oriented meetups or networking events are excellent venues to discover businesses seeking partnerships or investments.
- **Pop-Up Markets and Fairs**: Vendors at these events often run small businesses that are off the radar but have significant growth potential.

4. Your Daily Life

Keep a curious mindset during routine activities. Observe the businesses you frequent or pass by, and consider their potential.

Signs of Potential in a Local Business

Identifying a business with growth potential requires looking beyond surface impressions. Here are key indicators of a hidden gem:

1. Unique Offerings

Does the business provide something distinctive that sets it apart? Look for:

- **Specialized Products or Services**: Niche offerings that cater to specific customer needs.

> **Innovative Models**: Businesses that approach their industry in a fresh way, like eco-friendly laundromats or pet-friendly cafes.

2. Customer Loyalty

Repeat customers signal that a business is meeting a consistent demand. Signs include:

> **Busy Locations**: Regular foot traffic, even during off-peak hours.
> **Positive Reviews**: High ratings and glowing testimonials online or via word-of-mouth.

3. Market Gaps

Look for businesses that fill an unmet need in the local economy. Indicators include:

> **Limited Competition**: Few or no similar businesses in the area.
> **Growing Trends**: Industries experiencing increased demand, such as wellness services or plant-based dining.

4. Strong Community Connection

Businesses that actively engage with their communities—through sponsorships, partnerships, or events—often have a loyal base and potential for growth.

Networking With Local Entrepreneurs

Relationships are often the bridge to unseen opportunities. Networking with local entrepreneurs can open doors to partnerships, mentorship, or direct investment opportunities.

1. Where to Find Entrepreneurs

- **Business Networking Groups**: Organizations like BNI (Business Network International) often host local chapters.
- **Small Business Development Centers**: Many towns have centers that support entrepreneurs and host networking events.
- **Coworking Spaces**: Shared workspaces often attract ambitious, growth-minded business owners.

2. How to Build Connections

Networking is not about pitching yourself immediately but about forming genuine relationships.

- **Ask Questions**: Learn about their business, challenges, and vision for the future.
- **Offer Help**: Provide advice, connections, or resources to show you're invested in mutual success.
- **Stay Engaged**: Follow up regularly to maintain the relationship.

3. What to Listen For

Pay attention to conversations that reveal:

- **Businesses Seeking Growth**: Owners talking about expansion plans but lacking resources.
- **Challenges You Can Solve**: Opportunities to step in as an investor, partner, or consultant.

Learning the Needs of Your Local Economy

The best opportunities align with local demand. To find them, you must first understand what your community needs.

1. Research Local Trends

- **Economic Reports**: Check reports from your local government or chamber of commerce to understand economic strengths and weaknesses.
- **Community Surveys**: If possible, review surveys about residents' needs or interests.

2. Observe Consumer Behavior

- **Busy Spots**: Notice which businesses are thriving and why.
- **Unmet Needs**: Identify what people complain about or wish existed locally.

3. Engage with Residents

Talking to people in your community can provide valuable insights.

- **Ask Open-Ended Questions**: "What do you think our town could use more of?"

➤ **Participate in Forums**: Join local online forums or community meetings to gauge sentiment.

Matching Opportunities with Needs

Once you understand local demand, look for businesses that:

➤ Solve a widespread problem.
➤ Complement existing successful businesses.
➤ Have potential to scale as demand grows.

How to Evaluate a Business Without Financial Statements

Evaluating a local business's potential can seem daunting if formal financial data isn't available. However, you can gather valuable information through observation and dialogue.

1. Visit the Business in Person

➤ **Observe Customer Behavior**: Are people actively engaging with the business? Are they spending time and money there?
➤ **Assess the Atmosphere**: Does the business look well-maintained and inviting? A clean, organized space often reflects an owner's dedication.

2. Talk to the Owner

Engaging directly with the owner can reveal insights that financial statements can't provide. Ask questions like:

- "What's been your biggest challenge so far?"
- "Where do you see this business in the next five years?"
- "What makes your business stand out in this community?"

3. Gauge Community Sentiment

- **Customer Feedback**: Talk to regular customers about their experiences.
- **Reputation**: Look at reviews or ask around about how the business is perceived locally.

4. Assess Operational Strength

Even without financials, you can evaluate the operational health of a business by noting:

- **Staff Efficiency**: Are employees well-trained and productive?
- **Inventory Management**: Does the business seem well-stocked without being overstocked?

5. Consider External Factors

Understand the environment surrounding the business:

- **Location**: Is it easy to find and access? Does it have good foot traffic?
- **Competition**: How does it compare to other businesses in the area?

Key Takeaways

Finding hidden gems in your community requires curiosity, observation, and effort. By exploring directories, networking with entrepreneurs, and understanding the needs of your local economy, you can identify overlooked opportunities with significant potential. Even without access to formal financial data, you can evaluate a business's value by engaging with its owner, assessing its operations, and observing customer behavior.

The key is to stay open-minded, proactive, and persistent. Your next big opportunity might already be waiting for you, just around the corner.

Chapter 05
Doing Your Homework

Before diving into any local business opportunity, it's essential to conduct thorough research. Doing your homework not only helps you make informed decisions but also minimizes risks while maximizing your potential for success. This chapter provides a detailed guide on how to investigate a business, evaluate its environment, and use modern tools to your advantage.

How to Research a Business Thoroughly

Effective research begins with gathering a variety of information sources. By combining hard data with local insights, you can gain a well-rounded understanding of a business's potential.

1. Public Records

Public records offer a wealth of information about a business's history and operations. Key areas to investigate include:

- **Business Licenses**: Verify that the business is properly registered and in good standing.
- **Financial Health**: Some jurisdictions allow access to financial disclosures, such as tax filings or creditor reports.
- **Litigation History**: Search for any lawsuits or legal disputes involving the business or its owner.

Where to find this information:

- Local government websites.
- State Secretary of State's office.

- Online legal databases, such as PACER.

2. Customer Reviews

Online reviews provide firsthand accounts of customer experiences. While reviews are subjective, patterns can highlight strengths or weaknesses.

- **Look for Trends**: Are there consistent complaints about service, quality, or pricing?
- **Compare Ratings**: Check multiple platforms, such as Google Reviews, Yelp, and Facebook, for a broader perspective.

3. Community Input

Engage directly with local residents to gather informal but valuable feedback.

- **Ask Questions**: What do people like or dislike about the business?
- **Visit During Peak Hours**: Observe how busy the business is and how staff handle customer interactions.

Understanding the Competitive Landscape

A business's success doesn't exist in a vacuum—it depends on how well it performs relative to its competitors. Analyzing the competitive landscape helps you identify growth opportunities and potential threats.

1. Identify Competitors

- **Direct Competitors**: Businesses offering the same products or services in the same area.
- **Indirect Competitors**: Alternatives that fulfill similar customer needs but in different ways (e.g., a food truck vs. a sit-down restaurant).

2. Analyze Strengths and Weaknesses

Evaluate competitors based on:

- **Pricing**: Are they offering better value for money?
- **Customer Service**: Do they have a loyal customer base due to superior service?
- **Marketing Strategies**: Are they effectively attracting and retaining customers?

3. Identify Areas for Growth

Look for unmet needs or gaps in the market that the business could exploit.

- **Niche Focus**: Could the business specialize in a specific product or service?
- **Expansion Potential**: Are there underserved customer segments or geographic areas?

4. Competitive Differentiation

Ask yourself: What makes this business stand out? A strong unique selling proposition (USP) is a sign of potential.

Assessing the Owner's Track Record

The success of any business often hinges on its leadership. Understanding the owner's history, skills, and vision can provide crucial insights into the business's potential.

1. Past Experience

- **Industry Knowledge**: Has the owner worked in this field before?
- **Previous Ventures**: Were their earlier businesses successful or plagued by problems?

2. Management Style

- **Employee Feedback**: Speak with current or former employees, if possible, to learn about the work environment.
- **Community Perception**: Is the owner known for honesty, reliability, and professionalism?

3. Vision for Growth

A motivated and forward-thinking owner is more likely to lead the business to success. Look for signs of ambition and a clear plan for the future.

Spotting Risks Early

Every business carries risks, but understanding them upfront allows you to prepare effectively. Here are common pitfalls and how to identify them:

1. Financial Instability

- **Red Flags**: Excessive debt, inconsistent cash flow, or reliance on a few key customers.
- **How to Check**: Review bank statements (if available), analyze inventory turnover, and ask about outstanding loans.

2. Market Saturation

- **Red Flags**: Too many competitors vying for the same customer base.
- **How to Check**: Study the area's population, spending habits, and competitor density.

3. Operational Inefficiencies

- **Red Flags**: Poorly trained staff, outdated equipment, or disorganized processes.
- **How to Check**: Observe the business in action and speak with employees.

4. Regulatory and Legal Issues

- **Red Flags**: Unpaid taxes, lack of permits, or non-compliance with industry standards.
- **How to Check**: Consult public records and verify compliance with local regulations.

Practical Tools and Apps for Research

In today's digital age, technology makes it easier than ever to research businesses thoroughly. Here are some tools and apps to streamline your efforts:

1. Business Research Tools

- **Dun & Bradstreet**: Provides credit and financial information about businesses.
- **Glassdoor**: Offers employee reviews, useful for assessing management style and work culture.
- **Crunchbase**: Tracks small business funding and industry trends.

2. Market Analysis Tools

- **IBISWorld**: Offers in-depth market research reports.
- **Google Trends**: Tracks regional interest in specific products or services.
- **Census Bureau Data**: Provides insights into demographics and economic statistics for your area.

3. Competitive Analysis Tools

- **SEMrush**: Analyzes competitors' online presence, including website traffic and ad spend.
- **SpyFu**: Tracks competitors' keywords and search engine rankings.
- **Social Blade**: Measures social media performance, helping you assess their marketing strategies.

4. Local Insights Apps

- **Nextdoor**: A platform for hyper-local community discussions, often featuring small business recommendations.

- **Yelp for Business Owners**: Tracks reviews and feedback about local businesses.

Key Takeaways

Thorough research is the cornerstone of successful local business investments. By exploring public records, understanding the competitive landscape, and assessing leadership, you can identify opportunities with strong potential while avoiding common pitfalls. Use technology to streamline your efforts, but don't neglect the power of personal observation and community engagement.

Doing your homework isn't just about avoiding risks—it's about uncovering hidden value. Armed with the right information, you can confidently move forward, knowing you've built a solid foundation for success.

Chapter 06
Creating an Opportunity Funnel

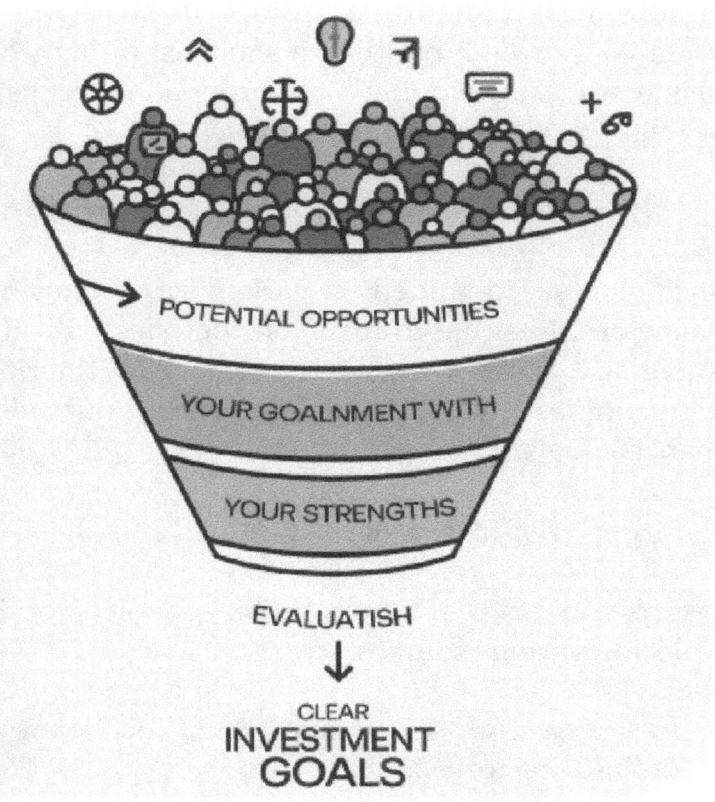

Turning a broad pool of potential opportunities into actionable decisions requires a structured approach. Creating an opportunity funnel allows you to systematically narrow down your options, evaluate alignment with your goals and strengths, and stay organized throughout the process. In this chapter, we'll guide you through building a short list of high-potential businesses, developing a criteria checklist, and establishing clear investment goals.

How to Narrow Down Your Options

Once you've identified a variety of promising local businesses, it's time to focus on the ones with the most potential. This process begins by filtering out opportunities that don't align with your vision or financial goals.

1. Start With a Broad Search

Ensure you have a comprehensive pool of options by exploring various sources:

- Businesses for sale listings (e.g., local newspapers, online directories).
- Recommendations from your network.
- Observations of thriving but underdeveloped businesses in your community.

2. Use Elimination Criteria

Filter opportunities based on deal breakers that make them unsuitable for your goals:

- ➤ **Location**: Is the business outside your preferred geographic area?
- ➤ **Capital Requirements**: Does it exceed your initial investment capacity?
- ➤ **Industry Fit**: Is it in a sector you're uninterested or inexperienced in?

3. Rank Opportunities by Potential

Assign a simple rating (e.g., 1-5) to each opportunity based on your initial impressions of its:

- ➤ Revenue growth potential.
- ➤ Customer demand.
- ➤ Operational efficiency.

Developing a Criteria Checklist

Having a clear checklist ensures that you evaluate all opportunities consistently. Your checklist should prioritize factors that align with your goals and risk tolerance.

Key Factors to Include in Your Checklist

1. Growth Potential

- ➤ Is the business in an expanding market or niche?
- ➤ Does the owner have a clear plan for scaling operations?
- ➤ Are there untapped revenue streams (e.g., e-commerce, additional locations)?

2. Community Fit

- How well does the business serve the local community?
- Does it have a strong, loyal customer base?
- Are there opportunities to increase community engagement?

3. Financial Viability

- Are the business's cash flows and profitability stable?
- Does it have manageable debt levels?
- Can it sustain itself during economic downturns?

4. Operational Strength

- Is the business well-organized, with efficient systems in place?
- Are the staff well-trained and customer-focused?
- Does it have a reliable supply chain?

5. Owner's Motivation for Selling

- Is the current owner retiring or pursuing a new opportunity?
- Is the business facing challenges that you feel confident addressing?

Evaluating Alignment With Your Skills and Interests

A business that aligns with your strengths and passions is more likely to thrive under your leadership. Playing to your skills and interests creates a sense of purpose and enhances your ability to manage challenges effectively.

1. Assess Your Strengths

- **Technical Skills**: Do you have expertise in the business's industry (e.g., marketing, operations)?
- **Leadership Style**: Are you comfortable managing people, setting goals, and driving performance?
- **Problem-Solving Abilities**: Can you address the business's pain points with confidence?

2. Consider Your Interests

- Does the business align with causes or hobbies you care about?
- Will it keep you engaged and motivated for the long term?
- Does it allow for creativity or innovation that excites you?

3. Match Skills to Opportunity

For example:

- If you excel in digital marketing, consider businesses with untapped online potential.
- If you're a strong communicator, look for businesses where customer interaction plays a critical role.

Setting Clear Investment Goals

Defining your investment goals is a critical step in narrowing your focus and guiding your decisions. A clear understanding of your "why" ensures that every choice supports your long-term vision.

1. Understand Your Motivation

Ask yourself:

- Are you seeking financial independence?
- Do you want to create a legacy for your family?
- Is this an opportunity to serve your community while earning a profit?

2. Define Success

Success means different things to different people. Be specific about what you want to achieve:

- **Financial Goals**: Set revenue, profit, or return on investment (ROI) targets.
- **Time Commitment**: Determine how much time you can dedicate to the business.
- **Personal Satisfaction**: Identify non-financial metrics, like work-life balance or community impact.

3. Break Goals Into Short-Term and Long-Term

- **Short-Term Goals**: Achieve profitability within the first 12 months, streamline operations, or expand marketing efforts.
- **Long-Term Goals**: Scale to new locations, double revenue within five years, or create a sellable asset.

How to Stay Organized While Prospecting

Managing multiple business opportunities can quickly become overwhelming. A well-organized system helps you stay on top of your research and ensures you don't overlook important details.

1. Use a Tracking Spreadsheet

Create a spreadsheet to track key information about each opportunity, such as:

- Business name and location.
- Owner contact details.
- Summary of key strengths and weaknesses.
- Financial highlights (e.g., revenue, profitability).
- Status of your evaluation (e.g., research complete, pending meeting).

2. Leverage Project Management Tools

Use digital tools to streamline your prospecting process:

- **Trello**: Create boards for each opportunity and track progress.
- **Asana**: Organize tasks, deadlines, and follow-ups.
- **Evernote**: Store notes, photos, and documents related to each business.

3. Schedule Regular Reviews

Set aside time weekly to review your findings, update your evaluations, and reprioritize your efforts.

4. Stay Connected

Maintain communication with business owners, mentors, and advisors to ensure you're gathering the most accurate and up-to-date information.

Key Takeaways

Creating an opportunity funnel allows you to systematically narrow down your options, focusing on businesses with the highest potential for success. By developing a detailed criteria checklist, evaluating alignment with your strengths, and setting clear investment goals, you'll be well-equipped to make informed decisions. Staying organized through tools and consistent reviews ensures that no opportunity falls through the cracks.

The goal is not just to find any business but to discover the right business—one that aligns with your goals, leverages your skills, and serves your community while providing financial rewards. This structured approach transforms prospecting into a strategic and rewarding process.

Part 3: Investing and Growing Wealth

Chapter 07
The Art of Making the Deal

Once you've identified a promising business, the next step is transforming that opportunity into a successful investment. This chapter explores the critical elements of making the deal: how to approach the business owner, structure a partnership, negotiate effectively, avoid mistakes, and formalize the agreement to protect your interests.

How to Approach a Business Owner

The way you approach a business owner can set the tone for the entire transaction. Building trust and demonstrating your value are essential to establishing a productive relationship.

1. Research Before You Reach Out

Come prepared with knowledge about the business and its owner. This shows respect for their time and establishes you as a serious prospect.

- Learn about the business's history, products, and challenges.
- Research the owner's background, such as their career achievements or community involvement.

2. Build Rapport First

Focus on building a connection before diving into business.

- ➢ **Be Genuine**: Show sincere interest in their story. Ask questions like, "What inspired you to start this business?"
- ➢ **Listen Actively**: Let them talk about their successes and challenges. Listening builds trust and gives you insights into their mindset.

3. Position Yourself as a Partner, Not Just an Investor

Emphasize the value you bring beyond money.

- ➢ Highlight your skills, experience, or network.
- ➢ Explain how your involvement could help the business grow, solve problems, or scale operations.

Structuring a Mutually Beneficial Investment

Every deal is unique, but successful investments balance the needs and goals of both parties. Structuring a partnership thoughtfully ensures everyone benefits.

1. Types of Investment Models

- ➢ **Equity Stake**: Buying a percentage of the business gives you a share of its profits and decision-making power.

- ✓ **Best for**: Long-term involvement with the potential for significant returns.

- ➢ **Revenue Sharing**: Instead of equity, you receive a percentage of monthly or annual revenue.

- ✓ **Best for**: Passive investors who want steady income without direct ownership.

- ➤ **Loan Agreements**: Provide capital in exchange for repayment with interest.

- ✓ **Best for**: Risk-averse investors seeking predictable returns.

2. Consider the Owner's Perspective

Understand what the business owner values most:

- ➤ Do they want to retain full control? Offer a passive investment model like revenue sharing.
- ➤ Are they seeking a strategic partner? Consider equity and active involvement.

3. Define Your Role Clearly

Set expectations upfront about your level of involvement:

- ➤ Hands-on: Participating in operations, offering mentorship, or managing specific areas.
- ➤ Hands-off: Limited to financial contributions and periodic check-ins.

Negotiation Tactics That Work

Negotiation is an art that requires preparation, empathy, and strategy. The goal is to reach an agreement that feels fair and beneficial to both parties.

1. Prepare Thoroughly

Know your priorities and deal-breakers before entering discussions:

- What is your maximum budget?
- What level of control or involvement do you require?
- What risks are you unwilling to accept?

2. Start With Common Ground

Frame the negotiation as a collaborative effort to achieve mutual goals:

- Use phrases like, "How can we structure this to work for both of us?"
- Focus on shared benefits, such as growing the business or solving operational challenges.

3. Be Willing to Compromise

Flexibility can help close the deal without sacrificing your core objectives:

- Consider alternative payment structures or timelines.
- Offer creative solutions, such as phased equity investments.

4. Keep Emotions in Check

Stay professional, even if the discussion becomes tense. Patience and a calm demeanor build credibility and trust.

Avoiding Common Mistakes in Negotiations

While negotiations can lead to exciting opportunities, they also come with risks. Recognizing red flags and avoiding common mistakes will save you from costly errors.

1. Overvaluing the Business

Owners may overestimate their business's worth due to emotional attachment.

- **Solution**: Use industry benchmarks and comparable sales to establish a realistic valuation.

2. Ignoring Hidden Costs

Consider expenses like deferred maintenance, inventory shortfalls, or underpaid staff.

- **Solution**: Conduct thorough due diligence to uncover hidden liabilities.

3. Failing to Define Roles Clearly

Ambiguity about decision-making authority can lead to conflicts.

- **Solution**: Specify roles, responsibilities, and expectations in writing.

4. Rushing the Process

Pressure to close quickly can result in poor terms.

- ➢ **Solution**: Take your time to review details and consult advisors if necessary.

5. Ignoring Cultural Fit

If your values or goals differ significantly from the owner's, the partnership may struggle.

- ➢ **Solution**: Ensure alignment during preliminary discussions.

Documenting the Deal Properly

A handshake agreement is not enough. Proper documentation protects your investment, clarifies responsibilities, and minimizes disputes.

1. Key Components of a Contract

- ➢ **Investment Terms**: Specify the amount, structure, and expected returns.
- ➢ **Roles and Responsibilities**: Define your involvement and authority in the business.
- ➢ **Exit Strategy**: Outline conditions for ending the partnership or selling your stake.
- ➢ **Non-Compete Clauses**: Prevent the owner from starting a competing business if they leave.
- ➢ **Dispute Resolution**: Include provisions for handling disagreements, such as mediation or arbitration.

2. Work With Professionals

- **Attorney**: Hire a lawyer experienced in small business contracts to draft or review agreements.
- **Accountant**: Ensure the deal is structured in a tax-efficient manner.
- **Consultant**: Consider a business consultant to verify the terms align with industry standards.

3. Protect Your Investment

- **Insurance**: Require the business to maintain adequate liability, property, and employee insurance.
- **Performance Milestones**: Tie funding or equity releases to measurable achievements, such as revenue targets.

Key Takeaways

The art of making the deal is about more than just numbers—it's about building trust, structuring win-win agreements, and ensuring all terms are properly documented. By approaching business owners with respect, preparing thoroughly, and negotiating strategically, you can create partnerships that lead to mutual success.

Remember: a good deal is one that aligns with your goals, protects your investment, and lays the foundation for long-term growth. Take your time, stay organized, and rely on professional advice to ensure every detail is handled correctly. When done right, the deal can be the first step toward building wealth and contributing to your community's prosperity.

Chapter 08

Managing Your Investment Effectively

Investing in a local business is only the beginning. To grow your wealth and support the success of the business, you need to manage your investment thoughtfully. This chapter focuses on understanding your role, adding value without overstepping, monitoring performance, addressing setbacks, and planning for a potential exit.

Understanding Your Role as an Investor

Your role as an investor can vary depending on your preferences, skills, and the needs of the business. Clarifying your level of involvement early ensures alignment with the business owner and avoids unnecessary conflict.

1. Hands-On Involvement

This approach involves direct participation in the business's operations or strategy.

- **Best For**: Investors with relevant expertise or a strong desire to influence the business's direction.
- **Examples of Contributions**:

  ✓ Offering guidance on marketing campaigns.
  ✓ Helping to streamline operations or improve efficiency.
  ✓ Mentoring the leadership team.

2. Hands-Off Involvement

This approach keeps your role limited to financial backing with minimal interference in daily operations.

- **Best For**: Investors seeking a passive income stream or who lack the time to be actively involved.
- **Key Actions**:

✓ Setting clear performance goals upfront.
✓ Receiving regular updates on business performance.

3. Hybrid Involvement

This balanced approach allows you to offer support and guidance when needed without taking on operational responsibilities.

- **Best For**: Investors who want some influence but trust the owner to handle most decisions.
- **Key Actions**:

✓ Attending quarterly strategy meetings.
✓ Acting as a sounding board for major decisions.

How to Add Value Without Micromanaging

As an investor, your goal is to empower the business owner while leveraging your skills and resources to foster growth. Striking the right balance ensures you add value without overstepping boundaries.

1. Leverage Your Expertise

Use your professional skills to support the business:

- **Marketing Knowledge**: Help craft campaigns or connect the business with a marketing expert.
- **Financial Acumen**: Provide guidance on budgeting, forecasting, or cost-cutting strategies.
- **Industry Insights**: Share relevant trends or best practices from your field.

2. Expand Their Network

Your connections can open doors to new opportunities:

- Introduce the owner to potential partners, suppliers, or clients.
- Connect them with mentors or consultants who can address specific challenges.

3. Provide Resources

Sometimes, small investments in tools or training can significantly impact the business:

- Offer funding for technology upgrades or employee development programs.
- Share access to software, subscriptions, or other resources you already own.

4. Respect Their Autonomy

While offering support, remember that the business owner is the primary decision-maker:

- Avoid dictating strategies or forcing decisions.
- Offer advice as suggestions, not mandates.

Monitoring Performance Without Overstepping

Regular monitoring helps you track the business's progress while maintaining a healthy partnership with the owner. Establishing clear expectations from the start ensures transparency and trust.

1. Set Key Performance Metrics (KPIs)

Agree on measurable indicators of success:

- **Financial Metrics**: Revenue growth, profit margins, or cost reductions.
- **Operational Metrics**: Customer satisfaction scores, inventory turnover, or employee retention rates.
- **Market Metrics**: Growth in customer base, online reviews, or social media engagement.

2. Schedule Regular Check-Ins

Maintain consistent communication without micromanaging:

- Monthly or quarterly meetings to review progress.
- Use a shared dashboard or report for easy access to key metrics.

3. Ask the Right Questions

Focus on understanding performance and identifying areas where you can help:

- "What's been your biggest challenge this quarter?"
- "Are there any resources or connections you need?"
- "What's your plan for addressing [specific issue]?"

Addressing Challenges and Setbacks

Every business faces hurdles, from declining sales to unexpected costs. As an investor, your role is to provide support and guidance while ensuring the business remains on track.

1. Diagnose the Problem

Encourage the owner to analyze the root cause of the issue:

- Is it external (e.g., market changes, competition)?
- Is it internal (e.g., staffing, operations)?

2. Collaborate on Solutions

Offer input without imposing your will:

- Brainstorm potential solutions together.
- Share examples of similar challenges you've encountered or read about.

3. Provide Tactical Support

Use your resources to help overcome obstacles:

- Connect the business with a specialist (e.g., HR consultant, marketing agency).
- Offer short-term funding to address cash flow gaps.

4. Stay Positive

Reinforce a solution-oriented mindset:

- Focus on what can be controlled and improved.
- Celebrate small wins along the way to rebuild momentum.

Planning for Exit Scenarios

Every investment should have a clear exit strategy. Whether you're scaling up or stepping away, planning for various scenarios ensures a smooth transition and protects your financial interests.

1. Define Your Exit Goals

Clarify why and when you would want to exit:

- **Financial Gain**: Achieving a specific ROI or selling at peak value.
- **Personal Reasons**: Shifting priorities, health, or time commitments.
- **Market Factors**: Declining growth prospects or emerging competition.

2. Common Exit Strategies

- **Sell Your Stake**: Transfer your ownership to another investor, the current owner, or a new partner.
- **Scale the Business**: Expand operations or enter new markets, then sell at a higher valuation.

- **Merge or Partner**: Combine the business with a complementary company to increase its value.

3. Preparing for the Exit

- **Strengthen the Business**: Focus on improving financial performance, customer retention, and operational efficiency to maximize its value.
- **Document Everything**: Maintain accurate records of financials, agreements, and operational processes to streamline the sale.
- **Consult Experts**: Work with attorneys, accountants, and business brokers to navigate the legal and financial aspects of the exit.

Key Takeaways

Effective management of your investment involves finding the right balance between support and independence. By understanding your role, adding value without micromanaging, and monitoring performance through open communication, you can foster a strong and productive partnership with the business owner.

Addressing challenges proactively and planning for exit scenarios ensures you remain adaptable and prepared for any outcome. Remember, your investment's success hinges on collaboration, clear goals, and the ability to adapt to changing circumstances. With these principles in place, you'll not only grow your wealth but also contribute to the long-term success of the business and its community.

Chapter 09

Scaling Up for Bigger Wins

Once you've successfully managed your first investment, the next step is to scale up and expand your portfolio. Growth brings exciting opportunities for bigger returns, but it also requires careful planning and strategic execution. This chapter explores how to identify the right time to expand, diversify within local markets, create synergies between businesses, build a reputation as a trusted investor, and grow sustainably without burnout.

When to Invest in Additional Businesses

Expanding your portfolio can multiply your wealth and influence, but timing is critical. Jumping into new investments too soon can stretch your resources, while waiting too long may mean missed opportunities.

1. Signs You're Ready to Expand

- **Your Current Investment is Stable**: The first business you've invested in is profitable and operates efficiently without constant oversight.
- **You Have Available Capital**: After ensuring an emergency fund and reinvesting in your current business, you have additional funds for new opportunities.
- **You've Gained Confidence**: Experience managing one business has honed your skills in evaluating opportunities, negotiating deals, and solving problems.
- **You Identify a Clear Opportunity**: You've spotted a local business or market gap that aligns with your expertise and goals.

2. Warning Signs to Wait

- You're struggling to manage your existing investment.
- You lack the capital to fund a new venture without overleveraging.
- You feel pressured to expand prematurely due to competition or external expectations.

Diversifying Within Local Markets

Diversification is key to reducing risk while growing your portfolio. By spreading your investments across various industries or business types, you can protect yourself against market fluctuations while capitalizing on multiple revenue streams.

1. The Importance of Staying Local

Expanding within your local market offers unique advantages:

- **Community Knowledge**: You already understand the demographics, spending habits, and cultural nuances of your area.
- **Existing Relationships**: Leverage your network of local entrepreneurs, suppliers, and professionals for support and opportunities.
- **Operational Efficiency**: Proximity makes it easier to oversee multiple businesses without excessive travel.

2. Diversification Strategies

- **Invest in Different Industries**: If your first investment is a retail store, consider exploring service-based businesses or manufacturing.
- **Target Different Customer Segments**: Cater to varied demographics, such as families, professionals, or retirees, to balance your risk.
- **Explore Complementary Businesses**: Choose businesses that align with your existing investments but operate independently, such as a bakery and a coffee shop.

3. Balancing Risk and Reward

Diversify cautiously by evaluating each opportunity's risk level, growth potential, and alignment with your long-term goals.

Creating Synergies Between Businesses

One of the most effective ways to scale up is by creating synergies between your investments. Synergies allow businesses to collaborate, share resources, and amplify each other's growth.

1. Sharing Resources

- **Staffing**: Cross-train employees to work across multiple businesses, reducing hiring and training costs.
- **Suppliers**: Negotiate bulk discounts by combining orders for shared materials or products.
- **Marketing**: Promote multiple businesses under one brand umbrella or through joint campaigns.

2. Cross-Promotion

Encourage customers of one business to support another:

- ➢ Offer bundled deals (e.g., a discount at a restaurant you've invested in with proof of purchase from your coffee shop).
- ➢ Use shared loyalty programs to incentivize repeat visits across your portfolio.

3. Collaborative Innovation

Businesses that share ideas can create unique offerings:

- ➢ A bakery and a café could collaborate on signature menu items.
- ➢ A fitness center could partner with a health-focused restaurant to host wellness events.

Building a Reputation as a Local Investor

As your portfolio grows, your reputation becomes a powerful asset. A positive track record attracts more opportunities, helps you negotiate better deals, and solidifies your standing in the community.

1. Deliver Consistent Results

Success breeds credibility. Focus on ensuring each business in your portfolio achieves:

- ➢ Financial stability.
- ➢ High customer satisfaction.
- ➢ Positive community impact.

2. Engage Actively in the Community

Show your commitment to the local economy and residents:

- Sponsor local events, schools, or charities.
- Join the local chamber of commerce or small business organizations.
- Mentor aspiring entrepreneurs or host workshops.

3. Share Your Success Stories

Build your personal brand by sharing your journey:

- Speak at local business events or community gatherings.
- Publish articles or blog posts about your experiences.
- Use social media to showcase the businesses you've supported and their impact on the community.

4. Foster Trust Among Entrepreneurs

Maintain ethical practices and treat business owners and partners with respect. Word of mouth spreads quickly in local markets, and being known as a fair, trustworthy investor will open doors to future opportunities.

Avoiding Burnout While Growing Your Portfolio

As exciting as expansion can be, it's essential to prioritize your well-being to avoid burnout. Balancing ambition with sustainability ensures you maintain the energy and focus needed for long-term success.

1. Delegate Effectively

As your portfolio grows, you can't manage every detail alone.

- Hire capable managers or partners to oversee daily operations.
- Outsource specialized tasks like bookkeeping, marketing, or HR.

2. Set Boundaries

Define limits on your time and involvement:

- Establish specific hours for meetings, research, and follow-ups.
- Avoid micromanaging by trusting the leaders you've put in place.

3. Focus on High-Impact Actions

Prioritize tasks and decisions that yield the greatest results:

- Spend time identifying high-potential opportunities.
- Focus on fostering strategic relationships and partnerships.

4. Schedule Downtime

- Take regular breaks to recharge and reflect.
- Pursue hobbies, family time, or activities unrelated to work to maintain balance.

Key Takeaways

Scaling up your portfolio is a natural progression for a successful investor. By recognizing when you're ready to expand, diversifying within your local market, and creating synergies between businesses, you can multiply your results while mitigating risk. Building a positive reputation strengthens your influence and attracts new opportunities, while prioritizing sustainability helps you avoid burnout.

As you grow, remember to stay grounded in the principles that made your first investment a success: clear goals, thoughtful planning, and a commitment to creating value for both businesses and the community. With the right strategies in place, scaling up can be an exciting and rewarding journey that propels you to even greater financial success.

Part 4: Long-Term Strategies for Wealth

Chapter 10

Building a Legacy Through Local Investments

True wealth goes beyond personal success. By strategically investing in your community, you can create a ripple effect that benefits generations, inspires others, and establishes a legacy that endures long after you're gone. This chapter explores the long-term impact of local wealth-building, including creating opportunities for others, being a role model, planning for succession, and giving back through philanthropy.

How Local Wealth Impacts Generations

1. The Ripple Effect of Investing Locally

Local investments don't just build wealth for you—they strengthen the economic fabric of your community.

- **Economic Growth**: Thriving local businesses contribute to a vibrant economy, increasing property values, tax revenues, and overall prosperity.
- **Community Stability**: When local businesses succeed, they anchor neighborhoods, providing consistency and pride.
- **Opportunities for Future Generations**: Today's investments create lasting infrastructure and job opportunities for tomorrow's leaders.

2. Inspiring Financial Literacy

Your journey as an unexpected millionaire can motivate others to adopt responsible financial habits. By openly sharing your success story, you encourage neighbors, friends, and even family members to explore investing and entrepreneurship.

Creating Jobs and Opportunities for Others

Local investments are powerful engines of job creation and economic empowerment. When you support a business, you don't just grow your wealth—you provide others with a chance to thrive.

1. Supporting Local Employment

Every successful business you invest in creates jobs for people in your community.

- **Direct Employment**: Hiring staff for operations, sales, and management.
- **Indirect Opportunities**: Creating demand for suppliers, contractors, and support services.

2. Empowering Entrepreneurs

Your investments can help other small business owners grow their ventures.

- Offer mentorship and guidance to inexperienced entrepreneurs.
- Provide seed funding or resources to startups that align with your community's needs.

3. Creating Pathways for Youth

Investments in local businesses can offer young people valuable opportunities:

- **Internships and Training**: Equip the next generation with skills and experience.

➢ **Educational Partnerships**: Collaborate with schools to support vocational training or entrepreneurship programs.

The Unexpected Millionaire as a Role Model

By building wealth through community-focused investing, you position yourself as a role model for others. This influence allows you to inspire others and foster a culture of possibility in your community.

1. Demonstrating the Power of Action

Your success shows that wealth isn't just for the privileged—it's achievable with hard work, smart decisions, and a commitment to community.

2. Sharing Your Story

Becoming a visible example of success can ignite change:

➢ Speak at local events, schools, or business forums.
➢ Publish articles, blog posts, or even your own book to share your journey.
➢ Use social media to highlight lessons learned and celebrate your community's growth.

3. Mentoring Others

Invest your time in guiding aspiring entrepreneurs or investors. Mentorship can multiply your impact by helping others follow in your footsteps.

How to Pass On Your Investments

Wealth that lasts generations requires careful planning. Structuring inheritance and succession ensures that your investments continue to benefit your family and community long after you're gone.

1. Structuring Succession Plans

A well-thought-out succession plan ensures smooth transitions:

- **Identify Successors**: Choose individuals who share your vision and values, whether they're family members, trusted partners, or key employees.
- **Provide Training**: Equip successors with the skills and knowledge needed to manage the businesses effectively.
- **Document Processes**: Maintain clear records of business operations, contacts, and strategies.

2. Inheritance Planning

Protect your wealth and streamline its transfer to future generations:

- **Establish a Trust**: Trusts can minimize tax burdens and provide clear guidelines for managing assets.
- **Write a Will**: Ensure your intentions are legally documented and easily understood.
- **Consult Professionals**: Work with estate planners and financial advisors to optimize your inheritance plan.

3. Family Involvement

Involve your family in your wealth-building journey early:

- Teach financial literacy and the principles of responsible investing.
- Invite them to participate in business discussions or decision-making.

Leaving a Philanthropic Legacy

Philanthropy is a powerful way to give back to your community and leave a lasting impact that extends beyond financial success.

1. Ways to Give Back

- **Scholarships**: Fund education for local students, particularly those pursuing entrepreneurship or vocational training.
- **Community Grants**: Support nonprofit organizations addressing issues like housing, health, or food security.
- **Infrastructure Projects**: Invest in parks, schools, or community centers that improve the quality of life.

2. Establishing a Foundation

Creating a charitable foundation allows you to formalize and scale your giving efforts:

- Define a mission that aligns with your values (e.g., supporting small businesses, fostering education).

➢ Involve your family or community in foundation activities to multiply impact.

3. Balancing Philanthropy with Profit

➢ Even while giving back, you can ensure sustainable wealth:
➢ Focus on social enterprises or businesses with a mission-driven approach.
➢ Support programs that generate long-term benefits for the community, such as workforce training or sustainable development initiatives.

Key Takeaways

Building a legacy through local investments is about more than personal wealth — it's about creating a lasting, positive impact on your community. By generating jobs, empowering others, and planning for the future, you ensure that your success benefits generations to come.

As an unexpected millionaire, your journey inspires others to believe in the power of local wealth-building. Whether you're passing on your investments to your family or giving back through philanthropy, your legacy will be defined not just by financial gains but by the lives you've touched and the community you've helped transform.

Your wealth is not the end goal; it's a tool for building a brighter future — for you, your family, and your community.

Chapter 11
Learning From Setbacks and Failures

Success in local investing is rarely a straight line. Setbacks and failures are inevitable parts of the journey, but they don't have to define your story. This chapter explores the common reasons local businesses fail, how to recover after a loss, and how to turn failure into a tool for growth. With the right mindset and strategies, you can emerge from challenges stronger and more prepared for future success.

Common Reasons Local Businesses Fail

Understanding why local businesses fail is essential for protecting your investments. While some failures result from external factors, many are preventable with foresight and proactive management.

1. Poor Financial Management

- **Cause**: Lack of budgeting, over-leveraging, or inadequate cash flow planning.
- **Solution**: Regularly review financial statements and implement sound accounting practices. Encourage the business owner to maintain an emergency fund for unexpected expenses.

2. Market Misalignment

- **Cause**: Selling products or services that don't meet local demand or ignoring customer feedback.
- **Solution**: Conduct thorough market research before investing and encourage adaptability to customer needs.

3. Operational Inefficiencies

- **Cause**: Outdated processes, untrained staff, or inventory mismanagement.
- **Solution**: Invest in staff training, technology upgrades, and streamlined systems to enhance productivity.

4. Lack of Differentiation

- **Cause**: Competing on price alone without offering unique value to customers.
- **Solution**: Identify and promote the business's unique selling proposition (USP) to stand out in the market.

5. Leadership Challenges

- **Cause**: Owners lacking experience, vision, or adaptability.
- **Solution**: Provide mentorship, connect them with resources, or consider replacing leadership if necessary.

How to Pivot After a Loss

A failed investment can feel devastating, but it's also an opportunity to regroup and come back stronger. The key to bouncing back lies in learning from the experience and applying those lessons to your next steps.

1. Assess the Damage

Take a step back and objectively evaluate the situation:

- **What Went Wrong?** Identify the specific factors that led to the failure.
- **What Could Have Been Prevented?** Determine whether red flags were overlooked during the investment process.

2. Shift Your Perspective

Reframe failure as a stepping stone:

- Recognize that every successful investor has faced losses.
- View the setback as a chance to refine your skills and strategies.

3. Develop an Action Plan

Focus on actionable steps to recover:

- Diversify your portfolio to mitigate risk.
- Pursue opportunities in industries or models where you've gained new insights.
- Build a financial cushion to prepare for future challenges.

4. Maintain Momentum

Avoid falling into inaction due to fear or doubt. Start small, rebuild confidence, and stay focused on long-term goals.

Reevaluating Your Approach to Risk

Every setback offers valuable lessons about your tolerance for risk and how to manage it more effectively in the future.

1. Reflect on Your Risk Assessment

Analyze whether you underestimated or misjudged risks:

- Were financial risks overlooked due to optimism?
- Did you rely too heavily on assumptions rather than hard data?

2. Adjust Your Investment Criteria

Use what you've learned to refine your approach:

- Prioritize due diligence, focusing on factors like financial health and market fit.
- Incorporate contingency plans for potential risks, such as industry downturns or unexpected costs.

3. Diversify Strategically

Reduce the impact of individual failures by spreading investments across different industries, business types, and risk levels.

4. Embrace Calculated Risks

Understand that no opportunity is risk-free. Instead of avoiding risk entirely, focus on making informed decisions with a balanced risk-to-reward ratio.

Finding Support During Tough Times

Recovering from a loss is easier when you have a strong support system. Seek advice, guidance, and encouragement from the right resources and communities.

1. Professional Resources

- **Financial Advisors**: Help you evaluate your portfolio and plan your next steps.
- **Business Consultants**: Provide insights into how to salvage or pivot struggling investments.
- **Lawyers**: Assist with legal aspects, such as disputes or contract renegotiations.

2. Peer Networks

Connect with other local investors who've experienced similar challenges:

- **Investor Groups**: Join local or online communities focused on small business investing.
- **Entrepreneur Meetups**: Engage with business owners to gain diverse perspectives.

3. Mentorship

Seek out experienced investors or entrepreneurs who can guide you through tough times. A mentor's insights can help you avoid repeating mistakes and regain confidence.

4. Emotional Support

Don't underestimate the psychological toll of a setback:

- Talk to trusted friends, family members, or a counselor.
- Practice stress-management techniques, such as mindfulness or exercise.

Embracing Failure as Part of the Journey

Failure is not the opposite of success—it's a critical part of it. Embracing setbacks as learning experiences helps you build resilience and become a more skilled and confident investor.

1. Shift Your Mindset

- View failure as a temporary setback, not a permanent state.
- Focus on the progress you've made and the knowledge you've gained.

2. Celebrate Lessons Learned

Take pride in the fact that you took action, even if the outcome wasn't ideal. Every experience adds to your expertise and prepares you for future opportunities.

3. Share Your Story

By openly discussing your setbacks, you:

- Help others learn from your experiences.
- Foster a culture of transparency and resilience in your community.
- Demonstrate that success is possible even after failure.

4. Reframe Setbacks as Stepping Stones

Each challenge you face equips you with tools to navigate future investments more effectively. Over time, your ability to adapt and grow will set you apart as a successful and enduring investor.

Key Takeaways

Setbacks and failures are inevitable in the journey of wealth-building. Understanding the common reasons for local business failure and learning how to pivot effectively after a loss are crucial skills for long-term success. By reevaluating your approach to risk, finding support during tough times, and embracing failure as a learning experience, you can turn challenges into opportunities for growth.

Remember, the path of an unexpected millionaire isn't about avoiding failure—it's about persevering through it. Every lesson learned adds to your resilience and expertise, bringing you closer to your ultimate goals. With the right mindset and strategies, each setback becomes a stepping stone toward even greater achievements.

Chapter 12

Celebrating Success and Staying Grounded

Reaching milestones on your journey as an unexpected millionaire is a significant achievement—but it's not the end of the story. In this final chapter, we'll explore how to celebrate success without losing momentum, maintain focus on your core values, and plan for the future while inspiring others through your story.

Recognizing Your Achievements

1. The Importance of Celebrating Milestones

Acknowledging your accomplishments is not just about patting yourself on the back—it reinforces motivation, builds confidence, and fosters gratitude for the journey.

- **Reflect on Your Journey**: Take time to appreciate the challenges you've overcome and the growth you've achieved.
- **Celebrate with Your Community**: Share your success with the people who've supported you, whether it's employees, partners, or family.

2. How to Celebrate Effectively

- **Mark Major Milestones**: Celebrate key achievements, such as hitting revenue goals, completing an expansion, or exiting a successful investment.
- **Reward Yourself Thoughtfully**: Treat yourself to something meaningful, like a vacation, a personal project, or an experience that brings joy.

- **Give Back**: Use your success as an opportunity to contribute to your community, such as hosting an event, making a donation, or supporting local causes.

Avoiding Complacency After Success

1. The Danger of Settling

Success can create a false sense of security, leading to stagnation or missed opportunities. Avoid complacency by staying curious, adaptable, and forward-thinking.

2. Strategies for Staying Proactive

- **Keep Learning**: Stay informed about market trends, emerging industries, and new investment opportunities.
- **Seek New Challenges**: Set ambitious goals that push you to grow further, such as diversifying your portfolio or entering new markets.
- **Stay Vigilant**: Regularly assess your investments to ensure they remain aligned with your goals and market conditions.

3. Balancing Ambition and Contentment

- Recognize that ambition and satisfaction can coexist.
- Appreciate what you've achieved while staying motivated to pursue new opportunities.

Staying True to Your Core Values

1. Wealth With Integrity

As your wealth grows, it's essential to ensure your actions align with your core values.

- **Community Focus**: Continue prioritizing investments and initiatives that uplift your local area.
- **Ethical Practices**: Maintain fairness and honesty in your business dealings.

2. Defining Success Beyond Wealth

True success is measured by the positive impact you create:

- Are you contributing to a thriving community?
- Are your investments creating opportunities for others?
- Are you living a life that aligns with your personal values and aspirations?

3. Setting Boundaries

As your influence grows, stay grounded by:

- Avoiding distractions that don't align with your mission.
- Saying no to opportunities that compromise your principles or spread you too thin.

Sharing Your Story With Others

Your journey as an unexpected millionaire can inspire others to pursue their dreams and build wealth in meaningful ways. Sharing your experiences also deepens your understanding of your own success and keeps you connected to your purpose.

1. Teaching Enhances Your Journey

Explaining your process to others forces you to reflect, refine, and improve your strategies:

- Mentoring young entrepreneurs helps you stay connected to emerging ideas and trends.
- Speaking at events or writing about your experiences reinforces your commitment to your values.

2. Ways to Share Your Story

- **Public Speaking**: Host workshops, panels, or local business forums.
- **Writing**: Contribute articles, blogs, or even a book that chronicles your journey.
- **Social Media**: Use platforms to celebrate milestones, share lessons, and connect with a wider audience.

3. Building a Legacy of Inspiration

- Encourage others to take their first steps toward wealth-building.
- Use your story to break down myths about success, showing that wealth is accessible to anyone with the right mindset and effort.

What's Next for the Unexpected Millionaire?

1. Evolving Goals

With your current achievements in hand, it's time to think about the next phase:

- **Scaling Your Impact**: Focus on investments or initiatives that create broader change, such as community development projects or industry innovations.
- **Exploring New Ventures**: Venture into industries or markets that excite you, even if they challenge you to learn something entirely new.
- **Planning for Future Generations**: Develop long-term strategies to pass on your wealth and ensure its positive impact endures.

2. Sustaining Personal Growth

Wealth-building is as much about personal evolution as financial gain:

- **Invest in Yourself**: Continue learning, whether through courses, mentorship, or travel.
- **Prioritize Well-Being**: Balance your professional ambitions with mental, emotional, and physical health.

3. Embracing the Journey

There's no final destination on the path to wealth — it's a continual process of growth, contribution, and exploration.

- Celebrate each stage of success while looking ahead to new possibilities.
- Embrace challenges as opportunities to learn and expand your capabilities.

Key Takeaways

Celebrating success is essential, but staying grounded and focused ensures that your achievements lead to lasting impact. By avoiding complacency, staying true to your values, and sharing your story with others, you create a legacy that extends beyond financial gain.

As you plan for the next phase of your journey, remember that wealth is not an endpoint—it's a tool for growth, empowerment, and contribution. Whether you're scaling up, inspiring others, or charting new paths, your role as the unexpected millionaire is to lead by example and use your success to make a difference.

The future is full of opportunities. Embrace it with gratitude, determination, and the knowledge that your journey has only just begun.

Conclusion

The Journey From Ordinary to Extraordinary

The path of the unexpected millionaire is not about luck or privilege—it's about recognizing opportunities, taking action, and staying committed to growth. Through this guide, you've learned the principles, strategies, and mindset required to transform ordinary circumstances into extraordinary success. Let's recap the key lessons, explore the limitless potential of local business investments, and offer a final push to help you begin your journey.

Recapping the Key Takeaways

The journey to wealth is built on actionable steps and a resilient mindset. Here are the most important lessons from this book:

1. Laying the Foundation

- Understand the local business landscape to uncover hidden opportunities.
- Embrace the power of community-driven wealth and the symbiotic relationship between businesses and their neighborhoods.
- Adopt a millionaire mindset by shifting from consumer to investor, embracing curiosity, and learning from failure.

2. Identifying the Right Opportunities

- Create an opportunity funnel to narrow down the best businesses to invest in.

- Evaluate potential investments with a checklist that considers growth potential, community fit, and alignment with your skills.
- Do your homework by thoroughly researching each business and its competitive landscape.

3. Investing and Growing Wealth

- Approach business owners with respect and transparency, negotiating deals that are mutually beneficial.
- Manage your investments effectively by monitoring performance, adding value, and planning for potential setbacks.
- Scale your portfolio thoughtfully by diversifying within your local market and leveraging synergies between businesses.

4. Long-Term Strategies for Wealth

- Build a legacy through investments that empower your community and create opportunities for others.
- Plan for the future with clear succession strategies and philanthropic goals.
- Celebrate your successes while staying grounded, focused, and committed to continual growth.

The Limitless Potential of Local Business Investments

Local businesses offer more than financial returns — they create a ripple effect of positivity that strengthens communities, uplifts families, and inspires others. Unlike impersonal investments in stocks or distant ventures, local businesses allow you to see the direct impact of your efforts:

- **Jobs Created**: Each investment supports livelihoods and fosters economic stability.
- **Community Enrichment**: Thriving businesses contribute to the vibrancy and identity of their neighborhoods.
- **Empowered Entrepreneurs**: Your investments enable passionate individuals to achieve their dreams, creating a cycle of inspiration and opportunity.

The potential for growth is everywhere—on your main streets, in your networks, and within your own ideas. All it takes is the willingness to look and the courage to act.

Your Role in Redefining Wealth

Wealth is more than money. It's the ability to create change, inspire others, and live a life aligned with your values. As an unexpected millionaire, you have the chance to redefine what success looks like for yourself and your community:

- **Shift the Narrative**: Show others that wealth isn't reserved for the privileged—it's attainable through hard work, smart decisions, and perseverance.
- **Make a Difference**: Use your financial success to uplift those around you, from supporting local causes to mentoring aspiring entrepreneurs.
- **Build a Legacy**: Create something that outlasts you, whether it's a thriving business, a philanthropic

foundation, or a community that benefits from your investments.

Your journey doesn't just redefine wealth for you—it inspires others to see new possibilities and strive for their own version of success.

Final Words of Encouragement

You don't need to be born into wealth, have advanced degrees, or possess a revolutionary idea to become a millionaire. What you need is the willingness to start where you are, with what you have.

- **Start Small**: Even modest investments or side businesses can lead to significant growth over time.
- **Stay Curious**: Opportunities are everywhere if you train yourself to look for them.
- **Be Persistent**: Every challenge you face is an opportunity to learn and grow stronger.
- **Give Back**: True wealth comes from making a difference in the lives of others.

Your journey from ordinary to extraordinary begins with a single step. Take it confidently, knowing that the path you're forging isn't just about wealth—it's about building a life of purpose, impact, and possibility.

The world needs more unexpected millionaires. Why not start with you?

www.ingramcontent.com/pod-product-compliance
Lightning Source LLC
Chambersburg PA
CBHW050312230526
45471CB00005B/2147